he's not a
mind reader

he's not a mind reader

{ And Other Brilliant
Insights for a Fabulous
First Year of Marriage }

A
GIRL'S
GUIDE

BRENDA GARRISON

Standard®
PUBLISHING

Cincinnati, Ohio

Published by Standard Publishing, Cincinnati, Ohio

www.standardpub.com

Copyright © 2010 by Standard Publishing

Also available: *Put the Seat Down and Other Brilliant Insights for an Awesome First Year of Marriage: A Guy's Guide* by Jess MacCallum, ISBN 978-0-7847-7462-5, copyright © 2010 by Jess MacCallum.

Printed in: United States of America

Editor: Laura Derico
Cover design: Ben Gibson
Cover illustration: © CSA Images
Interior design: Katherine Lloyd, The DESK
Interior illustrations: Jess MacCallum

ISBN 978-0-7847-2562-7

Library of Congress Cataloging-in-Publication Data
Garrison, Brenda, 1959-
  He's not a mind reader and other brilliant insights for a fabulous first year of marriage : a girl's guide / Brenda Garrison.
     p. cm.
  ISBN 978-0-7847-2562-7 (perfect bound)
  1. Wives--Religious life. 2. Newlyweds--Religious life. 3. Marriage--Religious aspects--Christianity. I. Title.
  BV4528.15.G37 2010
  248.8'435--dc22
                                        2010029139

15 14 13 12 11 10   1 2 3 4 5 6 7 8 9

For Gene

Thank you for being "my man."

With abundant thanks to the fabulous wives
who shared their funny, practical, and intimate marital stories
for this book. You blessed me to the core and I love you all.

contents

introduction

her man

"… and Wikipedia says he's monogamous!"

Her man. That is the way my grandma has always referred to someone's husband:

- "Her man worked on the farm."

- "Her man had a heart attack."

- "Her man was from Kansas."

But no matter what she says about "her man" or someone else's man, she says it with a measure of respect. With that measure of respect comes a certain way of treating her man and talking to him, and a certain set of expectations of him.

That respect is lacking in many marriages today—no matter the generation. Reflecting the typical wisecracking wife/bumbling husband image seen in almost every sitcom created since the invention of TV, women of all ages are treating their men like little boys, incompetents, or girlfriends. What's the big deal? The guys don't even notice or care, right?

Pause it right there.

Unlike the clueless men on TV, real men *do* notice. Next time you're in the presence of a woman disrespecting her man (of course, that won't be you!), just take a look at his face.

Women of all types are missing God's plan for wives to respect their husbands (Ephesians 5:33), and the blessings and benefits that come with that. The way we treat our men helps determine the kind of husbands they become. The wife whose comments to her husband are often "Do what I tell you" and "You never do anything right" may be tempting him to find someone who thinks he does a lot of things well. However, the wife whose comments to her husband are often "Thanks for helping with the dishes!" and "The lawn looks great!" may discover her man is a whole lot more understanding of her PMS, pre-PMS, and post-PMS.

As you enter your married life I want to share with you a few ideas that will show you how to help your man thrive in his role of husband and, as a result, in life. I've made lots of mistakes in my twenty-five years of marriage. But God gently shaped me into the wife that has helped Gene thrive as a fabulous husband.

Join me in my journey. Learn from my MANY mistakes. And then you might just hear people say:

⊙ "Her man is respected."

⊙ "Her man works hard."

⊙ "Her man treats her like a queen."

chapter one

the big, hairy man

"It's gone, Henry. It's gone."

I come from a family of all girls. My dad was the lone man in the house. When I married my husband, I had a lot to learn about men. Especially MY man.

Gene Garrison is a man's man. I tell others he isn't in touch with his feminine side because he doesn't have one. (Some of our friends have called Gene the manliest man they know.) He was raised on a farm. He is an ex-Marine. He is a construction guy. He doesn't wear sandals or use skin care products. Suits are for marrying or burying.

Well, you get the idea.

But don't get the wrong idea. He's got a heart of gold and will do anything for me or our girls. He's quiet at parties, but he makes me laugh like no one else can. We have a great marriage and it all started with . . .

Respect.

"You're the man, Gene (Dad). You're the big, hairy man!" You'll hear this often at my house. And it has absolutely nothing to do with my husband's personal grooming routine. It's what my daughters and I say when my husband exemplifies true manliness—when he does the gutsy thing or the hard thing no one else will, when he stands up for truth, or when he fixes something or tries to fix something. It's just our way of showing him respect and affirmation in fulfilling his role as provider, protector, and defender.

But I'm well aware this doesn't happen in everyone's house. The current culture and the women's movement have done their best to feminize and emasculate men. (Don't write to me explaining the women's movement. I was alive when it started. I know its positives and negatives. Positives: Extinction of the phrase *barefoot and pregnant* and getting women into some fierce footwear. Negatives: Birth of the "mommy wars.") As a result, men are confused about how to live out their masculinity and still not get smacked upside the head with a corporate-climbing professional woman's oversized Coach bag just for trying to open a door for her.

If that weren't enough to confuse a man about his identity, many such poor, male souls were raised by misguided matriarchs who refused to let their sons grow up and have modeled disrespect for their own husbands. They've shielded their sons from Dad's discipline. They've harangued their husbands on how to have a relationship with their sons because, well, of course those dads couldn't figure anything out on their own. Many of these moms have refused to acknowledge their sons as maturing young men or give them the respect due to them.

> { **Three Things to Do Every Day to Respect Your Man** }
>
> Tell him you love him (punctuated with a kiss or other form of physical affection).
>
> Do one thing that tells him you know him and love him (e.g., have his favorite beverage ready when he comes home; willingly give up the remote; wash, fold, and lovingly put back in his drawer his favorite, ratty, old T-shirt).
>
> Find a reason to cheer your man with your new mantra, "You're the man, you're the big, hairy man!" (And mean it!)

If you and your husband grew up with healthy role models, great! But if your guy didn't, he might not be accustomed to being shown respect. And if you were raised by a mother like the ones I described (and even if you weren't), you might not know how to show respect to *your* man (and you may need some counseling and TLC, too).

Respect is an attitude that permeates every area of the marriage. It is seen in everything we do for our husbands and everything we say about them and to them. As I mentioned earlier, Gene is a construction guy, so that means he is in the weather every day. When it's hot outside he comes home dripping in sweat and dirt. When it's freezing outside he has just begun to thaw out during his drive home. I show him respect by having either a cold drink (iced tea or milk-and-water—his own concoction) or hot coffee, depending on the weather, ready for him when he walks in the door. (Laugh if you like, but remember who's been married twenty-five years.)

We talk about our days. I am his number-one encourager and cheerleader as he tells me about the adventures and misadventures of the construction business. When respect permeates our marriages, our husbands will flourish as the men God created them to be and we too will be blessed.

I don't want to go any further in this chapter without introducing you to a friend. You may be intimidated by her or even cynical about her. It's OK. I used to feel the same way. Her story is told in Proverbs 31:10-31 and she is called "a wife of noble character." And after I got over my pride and really studied this gal, I learned that she is a role model. I am not mandated to accomplish every day everything described of her. She shows me what I can become over a lifetime.

Proverbs 31 talks about how a wife lives out respect and affirmation for her husband. "She comforts, encourages, and does him only good as long as there is life within her" (v. 12, *AMP*). Before you try to blot that verse out of your husband's Bible, remember what I said in the previous paragraph—the Proverbs 31 wife is our role model. No one can be all this all the time. However, the wise wife is the go-to girl for her man. He knows she is where he goes to be appreciated, encouraged, and understood. The wise wife protects her marriage by respecting her husband.

The benefits of a wife's respect are also discussed briefly in Proverbs 31. Her husband trusts her (v. 11). Oh, the problems in marriages that could be fixed if only there were trust! Her husband prospers and is respected by others (vv. 11, 23). A wife's respect and admiration can bring out the best in her man. He carries himself a little taller. He strives to do his best for her and to please her. He also praises her (vv. 28, 29). What woman couldn't use a little praise and admiration?

My friend's husband was in a stressful, demanding job with a boss who did not appreciate any of his efforts. Often her husband told her, "As long as I'm the hero in your eyes I can go out and do anything." My friend shared with me, "It's as if he is telling me, 'My self-worth and self-esteem come from you.'" She went on, "Guys don't care how many friends they have or who's doing what with whom. They just care if their wives think the world of them." Girls, if you want a man worthy of you, if you want your man to be ready to face the world, if you want him to be happy in his work, if you want him even happier to come home to you, you have the power to build him up and bring out the best in him.

The best thing you can do for your marriage is to respect, affirm, and appreciate your big, hairy man (even if he's short and balding). If he's not quite there yet, start building him up with respect. You will see him transform and you will be the one who benefits.

I'm very much a rubber-meets-the-road girl. I like to know exactly what someone is trying to tell me.

{ **Duct Tape Your Mouth If These Words Come to Mind** }

Why don't we just ask my dad?

You can't fix that. I'm calling _____. (Fill in the blank: Dad, Mom, the plumber, or—*gasp!*— my ex.)

Well . . . it looks good on Brad Pitt.

My mother said you'd be like this.

So at the end of every chapter I will give a few specifics so you can see how to or not to do this wife thing. The examples might not be suited to your specific situation, but you're a smart girl, you'll get the idea.

the SMART GIRL'S GUIDE **to Being Fabulous**

S mart girls can spell r-e-s-p-e-c-t in a number of ways.

⊙ *Never belittle him (especially in public).* And *never* share his secrets—not just the things he *tells* you to keep quiet, but the follies, foibles, and flub-ups that happen in the confines of your family life. Aubrey (married ten years) shared her wisdom with me. "It's a loyalty thing. I am surprised how women 'vent' about their husbands to anyone and everyone. He may not even know it, and certainly doesn't see or hear every instance where I abstain from joining in the husband bashing. Perhaps it doesn't directly build up our relationship, but indirectly it does. It cultivates an attitude of loyalty and an attitude in me that says *I'm on his side.*" Just think about it: how would you like it if you found out all your husband's friends knew you have been known to cuss like a sailor when you jam your big toe on the footboard of the bed?

⊙ *Get out of the way.* Most men won't fight their women for the role of leader (they shouldn't have to, either). When he's got a decision to make, express your opinion. Respectfully give your input. Ask questions. Then give him time to think things through and choose. Once guys are married, the weight of their responsibility hits them and they want to get it right. Give him the help he needs without becoming a roadblock.

- *Seek his input on your decisions,* even if they don't involve him. But I wouldn't ask how he would prefer the dishwasher to be loaded—he might just tell you.

- *Praise him for taking care of jobs around the house*, especially those that are outside his comfort zone. And be extra careful not to thwart his good intentions. One woman I knew came home from work only to find her husband had cleaned the living room . . . and put everything in a different place than what she would have chosen. The look on her face alone sealed her fate—four years later and he still hasn't attempted that job again. Poor woman. If only she had simply smiled and said, "Wow, honey, thanks for doing this!"

- *Praise him in front of others* for his latest accomplishment, whether it was in his work or in your home. Lisa, a young bride, learned this lesson the hard way. "We were in a small group setting and I made a comment about my husband not being technologically savvy with some piece of equipment. It truly embarrassed him and he was mad at me. . . . After almost seventeen years of marriage, I am aware of his sensitive areas and am very careful with what I say. Joking, teasing, or even mentioning a husband's weaknesses in front of others belittles him. Now I genuinely compliment him or affirm him in front of others when appropriate."

⊙ *Tell him you believe in him*, even when he's had a terrible, awful, bad, don't-even-want-dinner day, *and even when* you don't feel like it.

⊙ *Acknowledge the little things he does.* My wise, young friend Anne shared with me, "It took me a while to figure out that for me to just say 'Thank you for putting a new trash bag in the can' went a really long way toward him feeling loved and respected. I started our first year of marriage by disciplining myself every day to thank him for doing three things—even thanking him for 'minor' things like picking up milk and paying the bills—things he is 'supposed' to do anyways. It made me aware of how well he serves me, and to be grateful for him, thereby increasing my respect for him! Now it's just a regular part of our interaction."

⊙ *Respect his role as the provider.* Theresa's husband's long hours as a restaurant owner can easily become a source of irritation for her. She told me, "I don't always have a great attitude about his job, but I try to keep my mouth shut until the busy times pass. Instead of complaining about his job, I need to come alongside him, support his work, and be grateful that he is a passionate man who loves his family and his work. A few years ago when I decided to be more positive than negative about his work, I saw big changes in both of us."

chapter two

he's not
a mind reader

Some relationships are doomed from the start.

On a recent Sunday evening I was upset when my husband and I went to bed. Since I didn't want to let on to our fifteen-year-old daughter or keep Gene up, I went into our master bathroom to cry and pray. After about ten minutes Gene opened the door.

"Are you upset?" The lack of concern in his voice did not make me want to run to his arms.

"Why do you want to know?" I sniffed and glared at him with red, puffy eyes.

"What are you upset about *now?*" He proceeded to list a few issues I had chewed on over the weekend.

He still doesn't get me, came my superior female reasoning. This insight made me even madder—not only did he not have a clue what was causing me great distress, he thought I was holding on to things I had already dealt with and discarded.

"You think I'm upset about that stuff. That doesn't mean anything to me!" (*Sniff, sniff*—just the right amount of tears. Too many overwhelm and shut down most men.)

With that statement we both knew our pettiness was done

and I explained to him I was upset over a couple of situations with our older girls. Being my ever-faithful knight in shiny armor, he once again mounted his white horse and came to my rescue. "I'll talk to both of the girls and get this worked out." My hero!

You would think I would know better than to assume Gene knew how I felt. But no—I wanted Gene to *know* I was upset and *why*. Surely he could have figured it out, right?

Wrong. He knows me like none other, but he still can't read my mind.

We wives want our husbands to understand us. More than that. We want them to see inside us—to know when to draw us out, and when to let us brood. We want them to know that even though we said, "That purse is too expensive," we really mean "Go back and get it." We want them to know not only what we are mad about but *why* we are mad—yep, men don't usually get the *why*.

However, our men are mere mortals, not mind readers. Any mind-reading superpowers your husband seemed to have when you were dating are long gone. Who knows—maybe the motivation is not as strong or, more likely, your conversations are less clouded now by romantic bliss, but for whatever reason, that kiss at the altar seems to have sapped all the intuition out of him—at least where your inner thoughts and feelings are concerned.

No longer does he know how you feel about what your sister said to you. Nor can he sense that you are nervous about your job interview—even when you start chain-smoking and eating Moose Tracks ice cream . . . at the same time. He doesn't understand why you can't settle on one stupid dress for his stupid high school reunion (you saw his old girlfriend on Facebook).

And he won't know these things unless you tell him. He wants to know these things—OK, maybe not all of these things. But he definitely wants to know you. It's just that he'll never understand you. That is not a man-slam. It's just the truth. Men are wired differently than women and parts of our minds—the female parts—will never make sense to them, no matter how many tears we shed or hours we spend or aspirins we take to get rid of the headaches we get when we try to explain ourselves to them.

And let's face it—we're not mind readers either. We may be better at remembering what we know about them, or perhaps we may be slightly more adept at feigning interest in their obsessions. But that doesn't mean we understand *why* he can only wear one kind of socks or *why* he likes the movies he does or *why* he gets angry and sarcastic every time he's sad.

So what should you do? Invest in plush bathroom furnishings so at least you have someplace comfortable to hide and cry? Just because we think and feel differently doesn't mean we can't have meaningful communication and deeper connections. We need to learn to communicate in a way that works for both us and our husbands.

Start by studying your man. Most men have four limiting factors in common when it comes to listening to women: 1) limited endurance; 2) distracter factors; 3) shutdown switches; and 4) guy-defined goals. First, most men come with an automatic timer—they can only listen for so long in a particular day or sometimes even during a particular conversation. How and when is your guy most attentive? Second, most men have certain things that will suck their attention away from you at a moment's notice—whether it be their latest gadgets, hunger, the news, or their favorite commercial. Be mindful of your guy's distracter factors

{ Duct Tape Your Mouth
If These Words
Come to Mind }

You should *know* why!

You never want to talk to me. Why don't you ever want to talk to me? Why? Are you listening? You're not listening! You never understand me!

Shut up! I'm trying to talk to you!

Not now. *What Not to Wear* is on.

and save your breath. Third, most men have particular triggers or switches that will cause an immediate conversation shutdown. For some it's tears, for others it's tones of voice, for others it's words like "you never," "I feel," or "female troubles" and "craft store."

This may be a rather painful learning curve, but pick up on your husband's triggers and avoid them, if you can. And lastly, most men approach communication with guy-defined goals—usually involving fixing something or finding a solution or getting to the point. Crazy things like that. These goals will often not fit your needs. So you'll have to work together to figure out the best way to get what you want out of your exchanges. But realizing what his goals are is half the battle.

Here's an example of what I'm talking about. When Gene comes in the door after work he immediately starts shuffling through his pile of mail and my notes for him. He fires off half-questions and comments: "What's this?" and "I already saw this" and "What's in here?" The reason these are half-questions and comments is because only half of his brain is engaged—the other half is still at work. This used to drive me crazy. I finally figured out that, when Gene comes home, he needs

> **Three (or Four) Things to Do Every Day to Improve Communication**
>
> Give him your total attention when he talks about his day.
>
> Overlook one (or two) of his thoughtless comments (see 1 Peter 4:8).
>
> No more nagging—use a sticky note, a text, or frosted writing on a cinnamon roll to remind him of dinner with your parents or to pick up the milk.
>
> Laugh at his jokes.

some downtime to transfer his thinking from work to home. So now when he starts this, I sweetly say, "Let's talk about it in a few minutes." By giving Gene time to transition, he is alert and ready to deal with the business of our home. I am less frustrated with his after-work ADD, and we have better communication and a more enjoyable evening.

My mom used to tell me, "It's not what you say, but how you say it." Gene has often agreed with her. I am passionate and *sometimes* bossy. This combination can come across as harsh (did I mention how passionate I am?), especially to a man who did not get married to be bossed or lectured. He had enough of that in the Marines.

God used two verses from Proverbs to get my attention and take off my rough edges. Proverbs 15:1 spoke directly to my tone, "A gentle answer turns away wrath, but a harsh word stirs up anger." My to-the-point, no-holds-barred tone unnecessarily agitated Gene. Then God hit me with the warning of what would happen if I didn't change my tone. "The wise woman builds her house, but with her own hands the foolish one tears hers down" (Proverbs 14:1). Yikes! I had the power to build up my man, home, and family, but I also had the power to destroy it all. Now *I* was the one who had to polish my listening skills. I started listening to God when he showed me the edge on my words, then I chose my words more wisely. I also learned to relax my tone and give my husband time to respond.

Communication may be difficult sometimes, but it's never impossible. Unlike mind reading. Or understanding why fifteen minutes in football takes three hours.

the SMART GIRL'S GUIDE **to Being Fabulous**

S mart girls learn the finer points of male/female communication.

- ◉ *He's not your girlfriend, so don't expect him to be.* If you want to talk something into the ground, call a girlfriend. In the story I shared at the beginning of the chapter, if I would have gone on and on with female detail, Gene would have shrugged his shoulders and gone back to bed. But since I fairly concisely shared my feelings and the cause, he was able to come up with a way to help.

- ◉ *For the times you don't want help, tell him that first: "I just need to process."* My friend Amelia and her husband Jack have worked this out. "Basically, like most women, I am a verbal processor. And Jack, like most men, is a problem-solver. So early in our marriage, I would be 'processing' and he was feeling overwhelmed and frustrated by me contradicting myself while I talked, not making sense (to him), rabbit-trailing as I went. He couldn't keep up, and therefore didn't feel like he could either understand me or help me. So we learned that I would preface a 'processing session' by letting him know I was just needing to process, and I actually gave him permission to zone out during the first 75 percent of what I was going to say—and then, when I felt like I had come to a more succinct conclusion, I would say his name and then he knew to pay attention. That way, it minimized frustration on both our parts, and he didn't have to feel badly for not really paying attention—because I had given him permission not to. And yet, we both knew that when I got down to the nitty-gritty, he was fully there."

◉ *Not to overstate the fact, but HE'S NOT A GIRL.* Don't expect him to feel and react the same way you do. Especially during hard times—loss of a job, friend, or child—give him room to work through the situation. Anne and Jeremy were expecting their third child. One test led to another and the diagnosis was given that this baby girl would not live. She went into the arms of Jesus six hours after birth. Anne and Jeremy processed and dealt with her diagnosis and home-going very differently. At the end of a lengthy e-mail explaining their personal journeys, Anne concluded, "In a nutshell? I chose an avenue of quiet, solitary meditation, and Jeremy chose an active pursuit of answers to the questions he had in his heart. And God met each on our own path, and has brought us to a better understanding of him, ourselves, and each other as a result."

◉ *Connect the dots for him.* If you had an awful day at work and would like for him to pick up dinner, here's what you do: call or text him and tell him you had an awful day at work and would like for him to pick up dinner. Again, men aren't mind readers and they don't like for us to assume they are. Most husbands love to please their wives—they just need a few ideas. OK, lots of ideas. Speaking of ideas—give your husband a list of what you would like for your birthday or Christmas. Include size, color, and store or Web site. Our first Christmas required knee-jerk grace on my part. Gene bought me a blouse—striped with a self-tie bow. It could be argued that it was in style, but it wasn't *my* style. Lesson learned.

⊙ *Give him a chance to talk.* Ask him about his day—more than "How was your day?" Ask about details and events. Let the conversation lull so he can share what's on his mind. Don't over-respond when he shares. Affirm his thoughts. Remember, you want to be his go-to girl for respect and affirmation. He doesn't need to look elsewhere. He's got it all in you.

chapter three

reality romance

Victoria's Other Secret

Valentine's Day, 1985. Newlyweds Gene and Brenda celebrate their first Valentine's Day as a married couple by sanding the doors of their kitchen cabinets. Then they go to McDonald's for dinner.

OK, so maybe that's not exactly a newsworthy way for a romantic couple to spend the day, but for us, it was exactly what we wanted to do—work on the remodel of our old farmhouse. It was symbolic of the new life we were building together.

Romance in marriage is as varied as each married couple. There is no right or wrong way to do it.

But before we go on, let's stop for a reality check: what chapter are we in? Three, right? And where's the sex chapter? Seven. Yep. Romance and sex are totally separate—we planned it that way. The fact is, though many times (especially but not only early in marriage) romance does lead to sex, as life changes take place, that is not always possible. *Gasp!* I know. It's OK. Breathe. Now listen to me.

Your life will not always be as it is now. One of you may need to travel often for work. Children, even many children, may present schedule difficulties. (I may just win a prize for that last sentence—Understatement of the Millenium.) One of you may develop a chronic illness. (Are you depressed yet?) You have no idea what will happen in your life. So eating dinner in your lingerie (with your hubby for dessert) won't always be a possibility. However, that does not mean that romance should be neglected. Creative romance plays a crucial role in keeping the relationship strong and thriving—in keeping you husband and wife, not just partners sharing a house, kids, and a dog. In the changes and craziness of life, romance is essential for the health of the marriage.

{ Romance May Be on Vacation in Your Marriage If . . . }

Your last loving words to your man were "I do."

When you come home you kiss the dog and pat your husband's head.

The only notes/e-mails/texts you sent your husband in the past month were to remind him to pay the phone bill and pick up the kitty litter.

So now that we've got that straight, let's examine a working definition of romance. The best definition I found defines romance as: "ardent emotional attachment or involvement between people" (http://dictionary.reference.com/browse/romance). We want to nurture our marriages by keeping the "ardent emotional attachment" strong and growing between us and our husbands.

A few years ago Gene and I were at a pool party. (If you're like me you now have the unsettling image in your head of a flock of forty-something and fifty-something folks wearing swimsuits. Rest easy—the adults were wearing casual summer attire and the *kids* were swimming. Back to my story.) I glanced around the group and a married couple, friends of ours, caught my attention. I couldn't hear what they were talking about, but as they were finishing their conversation, each took a step away from the other, heading in different directions. I don't remember if they had been holding hands, but I noticed as the wife said one more thing to her husband, they loosely linked their fingers. They stood about two feet apart with fingers entwined gently for that one last thing she wanted to tell him. They looked natural and totally comfortable—at home. I remember thinking, *They are joined at the heart.*

This couple is a few years ahead of Gene and me on the marriage journey. They have been through their trials. They aren't overly touchy with each other in public. But this subtle gesture of holding onto each others' fingers as the last words were spoken showed anyone with eyes to see it that their relationship (including the physical part) was strong and thriving. To me *that* was romantic.

Romance is a vital component of your go-to girl kit. Suppose you text your hubby while he is at work, telling him one thing you love about him or one thing you find attractive about him. A satisfied smile comes to his lips. "What's up with you?" chides his coworker. In just a few seconds, you've supercharged his manhood and become a focal point in his mind for the rest of the day. No matter what saucy, underdressed woman walks by him, his mind is already on getting home to you. You are his prize—his go-to girl for romance.

I must confess the only book of the Bible I have read less often than Revelation is Song of Songs (also known as Song of Solomon). I guess I think: *Yeah, yeah, I know. Marital sex is good—got that covered.* So I don't look to that book for life instruction as I do the rest of the Bible. But I've been missing out!

Song of Songs, especially chapters one and two, show how a woman who romances her husband thinks and lives it in their relationship. The Shulammite woman wears perfume to keep herself in his mind (1:12, 13). (This wouldn't work for me because Gene does not have a sense of smell. The homemade bread and cookies that I put in his lunch do the trick!) She compliments his appearance ("How handsome you are, my lover! Oh, how charming!") and lets him know she has made preparations for a romantic evening (1:16, 17). She looks forward to their time together and is ready to respond to him (2:8-13):

> Listen! My lover!
>> Look! Here he comes,
>> leaping across the mountains,
>> bounding over the hills.

> My lover is like a gazelle or a young stag.

. . .

> "Flowers appear on the earth;
>> the season of singing has come,
>> the cooing of doves
>> is heard in our land.

> The fig tree forms its early fruit;
>> the blossoming vines spread their fragrance.
>> Arise, come, my darling;
>> my beautiful one, come with me."

All right. So maybe your husband would prefer NOT to be called a gazelle and maybe you can't say you've heard the "cooing of doves" in your land. I know these examples are over two thousand years old, but think about it. This woman may have been the only woman to capture the heart of the wisest man who ever lived, King Solomon (Charles C. Ryrie, ed., *The Ryrie Study Bible, New American Standard Translation* [Chicago: Moody, 1976, 1978], 1000). Solomon compared her to his other wives and concubines, "But my dove, my perfect one, is unique" (6:9). Surely we can learn something about romance from the Shulammite woman—she knew how to capture the heart of her man and she had way more competition than we will ever have (unless, of course, you count the Internet)!

{ **Romance Trade Secrets from the Voice of Experience** }

Plan to spend the whole day secretly flirting with one another.

Arrange a special date or getaway day, keeping the destination and plans secret from your husband.

Take a quote from a favorite TV show, movie, book, or song you share with your husband and use it as code for a special message between the two of you. So every time you say "Use the Force," you really mean "Kiss me now."

Figure out what will make your guy say "I'd marry you again!" instead of "What was I thinking?" Then do it.

S mart girls figure out the best ways to keep romance alive.

⊙ *Keep connecting.* Since Gene leaves for work between 4:30 AM and 5:00 AM, our only time to enjoy a morning cup of coffee together is on the weekends. We make it a priority to get up before the kids and have coffee and conversation. This is our chance to really talk, not only catching up on the week, but sharing more deeply. I enjoy this, of course, but Gene has often told me how special this time is to him.

⊙ *Keep up your appearance.* We will talk more about this in the next chapter, but this speaks romance to my man. One of my friends and her husband said the same thing when asked about romance. "I always try to dress nice for my man. He has told me that it is important to him and that he appreciates that I do so! When I go shopping it is always at the forefront of my mind: *Will he like me in this?*"

Recently I lost the few pounds I have struggled with for over a year. My youngest daughter and I were shopping for new jeans. I tried on a pair that fit like they were made for me. The look on Kerry's face said

Wow! Those jeans look bad on you! and she expressed that (*bad* being a good thing here). She was right. Even though they were a few dollars more than I usually spend on jeans, I bought them. Gene told me to get a second pair!

⊙ *Keep the signals going.* E-mail, text, or leave voice mail messages during the day or when you're apart. Gene and I often call during the day—the subject matter may be silly, but the connections are significant. It's like the perfume in Song of Songs 1:12, 13—a constant reminder of his loving wife anticipating their time together.

⊙ *Keep away from romance killers*—no nagging!

⊙ *Keep touching*—not sexually, but lovingly, like my friends who linked fingers during their conversation. A little kiss or hug. Sometimes I give Gene a quick smack on the bottom when he walks by. (I know he loves it!) Rub your husband's head, scratch his back, or put your hand on his knee while you're watching a movie. If physical affection doesn't come naturally to you, put it on your to-do list every day. A little romance might just turn your to-do list into a ta-da list!

chapter four

it's your body,
but he gets to look at it

"Well, of course I married you for your figure!"

Gene often says two words as he draws me close and looks deeply in my eyes. "Thank you."

"For what?" I never know what's coming.

"For taking care of yourself. It means a lot to me."

Apparently it means a lot to lots of other men, too. In her book *For Women Only: What You Need to Know About the Inner Lives of Men*, Shaunti Feldhahn writes that "seven out of ten men indicated that they would be emotionally bothered if the woman in their lives let herself go *and didn't seem to want to make the effort to do something about it.*" She goes on to clarify, "But over and over again, I heard each man say that what mattered most to him was not that his wife shrank down to her honeymoon bikini, but that she was willing to make the effort to take care of herself for him" (Colorado Springs, CO: Multnomah Publishers, 2004, 161, 162).

I have never been a size 2. I have almost always struggled to keep my weight under control. (Except immediately after Katie's birth when my thyroid went nuts and I could eat whatever I wanted and not gain a pound!) At 5'8" I carry more weight than most would guess, so what I'm talking about in this chapter is not about being thin. I'm talking about the whole package—our total appearance and our mental, emotional, and spiritual well-being. Taking care of all these areas enables us to help our men and marriages thrive because *we* are thriving. We can be a blessing to our husbands—confident and fun to be with.

Let's take a quick look at a couple of wives in the Bible that took care of themselves and were blessed because of it. First we'll revisit our friend and role model, the Proverbs 31 wife. Verse 22 tells us that "her clothing is fine linen and purple." The word for linen here means silk (James Strong, *Strong's Exhaustive Concordance of the Bible* [Chattanooga, TN: AMG], 161, Hebrew and Chaldee Dictionary of the Old Testament). Purple is the color for royalty or the rich. This woman dresses well. And apparently she is staying in the family's budget, because "her husband has full confidence in her" (v. 11), "she brings him good, not harm" (v. 12), and he praises her (vv. 28, 29). She is doing a good job of looking good.

{ **Yes, There Are Stupid Questions** }

Does this make me look fat?

Do you think she's pretty? (*she* being any celebrity, friend of yours, or the neighborhood beauty queen)

How much do you *think* I weigh?

If you could change any part of me, what would it be?

Let's also peek in on the lovebirds again, King Solomon and his wife, the Shulammite woman. In chapter four King Solomon goes on and on about the beauty of his wife. He appreciates every part of her appearance—even her teeth! Who says men don't notice when we try to look nice? (Of course, it probably didn't hurt that she was most likely naked except for a thin veil. Try that look out at home, ladies!)

Perfection is not required, but we do need to try, and keep trying—even when we're feeling more bloated than blooming, or perhaps especially then. Shaunti Feldhahn shared a comment from one of her male friends: "But then sometimes I'll meet a man whose wife is overweight—but she takes care of herself. She puts some effort into her appearance. She dresses neatly, or does her makeup and hair. If she is comfortable in her own skin and is confident, you don't notice the extra pounds. I look at that husband and think, *He did well*" (*For Women Only*, 169).

{ **Run Out and Buy** *InStyle*, *Vogue*, and *Newsweek* If . . . }

You find yourself buying pants with elastic in the waist.

You run into friends from high school and they instantly know your name because you truly "haven't changed a bit!"

You think you're getting all the current events you need from status updates on Facebook.

Our physical appearance isn't the only part of us we need to take care of. Our husbands will greatly appreciate brains to go with our beauty. In his book *So Much More Than Sexy*, Mark Atteberry tells women like it is. "Face it. A good guy falls for and sticks with a woman who has some depth. There's nothing he loves more than to be attracted to a woman he thinks is beautiful, only to discover there's even more to her than he could see. On the other hand, one of the most disappointing moments in a man's life is when he's attracted to a woman he thinks is gorgeous, only to discover there's much *less* to her than he had hoped" (Cincinnati, OH: Standard Publishing, 2009, 75).

You are full of ideas! Stay that way! Read (and not just your favorite dog-eared novels or magazines—try something he might like too). Listen to the news—objectively and don't believe everything you hear. Process it, compare it with God's Word, discuss it. Continue your education. Get involved in a meaty Bible study. Then talk, talk, talk to your man. And listen to him, affirming him. Remember you want to be his go-to girl in all areas.

When my daughters were in high school and frustrated because they weren't dating, I used to tell them that the boys were just not ready for them yet. My girls were pretty, smart, and confident—and still are! Their guys needed time to mature and build their own confidence. Well, girls, your guys are ready. They bought the ring, said the magic words, and told God and everybody that you're the one. Don't let them down now.

the **SMART GIRL'S GUIDE** to Being Fabulous

S mart girls care for their husbands by taking care of themselves.

⊙ *Take time with the Lord.* A vital and growing relationship with God enables us to be the best we can be in all areas of our lives. My precious friend Mandy lost her husband when he was too young. She just celebrated her second wedding anniversary with her new husband, and she shares, "This is an ongoing endeavor, always something that I need my God's help on in smoothing out my rough edges! . . . Here I am, forty-eight years old, in a new relationship, and I thought I knew myself really well, and yet there are some not so pretty things lately that have raised their ugly heads and taken me by surprise! Ahhh! How creative of God to bring an outstanding new man into my life to bring these things to the surface evidently from the deepest darkest crevices within me."

⊙ *Take care of yourself physically.* Start with personal hygiene. I'm not your mom and I shouldn't have to say this, but I have a feeling I must. Take a look in the mirror. When was the last time the eyebrows were tamed? hair washed? Are your legs as hairy as your husband's? How about your nails? Professional manicures are not my style, but keeping nails clean and filed always looks nice.

- *Take time to find your style.* No, pajama pants are not a style. Get your act together, girl. Wear clothes that fit—not too tight, nor too loose and baggy. Be considerate of your husband's preferences as well. One wife confided in me, "I do not wear high heels because Tom and I are about the same height and he really doesn't like it when I am taller." It matters to her husband, so she keeps to a kitten heel.

- *Take it easy on yourself.* I have never met a woman who loved everything about her body, so let's admit it and deal with it. No matter what part of your body you wish were different, accept it and love it. Dress it in a way that flatters it. I love the cable show *What Not to Wear*. It helps women of all shapes dress beautifully. Don't forget—your husband married you so he already *loves* your body.

- *Take time for girlfriends.* Your husband has probably already noticed the emotional release you get when you are with *good* friends. A few years ago a friend of mine went through an extremely hard time. All through it a core group of women stood by her, each doing her part to encourage and support her. When the situation was resolved, she hosted a beautiful luncheon for us. The centerpieces were bouquets of white roses. My friend explained how she justified the price of the bouquets to her husband, "I told Steve that white roses were cheaper than therapy!" Her friends' friendships carried her through.

◉ *Take time for healthy routines.* We feel better when we exercise and eat right. Believe me, when we get to chapter seven you'll be glad you're keeping in shape! Find what works for you.

chapter five

wilma flintstone got something right

"Honey, I don't mean to be critical, but next time
could you kill something that matches?"

Afew years ago a young wife asked me to mentor her. She wanted to take care of her husband, but did not have a clue how to start. Her first question: "I don't know how to serve him. He does everything for me, but what can I do for him?"

"What about breakfast? Do you get up with him and make breakfast?" I thought it best to start at the beginning.

"No, but I will."

The following week she asked him if he would like her to make breakfast.

"No. I don't do breakfast. All I want is coffee."

We met a few days later. "Now what? He drinks coffee till lunch." She was stumped.

"What about dinner? Do you cook dinner?" It seemed logical.

"No. I don't know how." Her giggle said *I know I should know.* But she couldn't know. Home-cooked meals were not a part of her growing-up years.

So she asked her husband, "Would you like me to cook dinner every night?"

"Yeah. That would be great."

Yes! She discovered one way she could take care of her man. She did not know how to plan a meal, shop for groceries, or cook, but those were easy fixes.

In my book *Queen Mom* I state, "Moms are the heart of the home. In fact, we set the mood in the home. We keep communication flowing in our families. We provide a safe, comfortable haven for our families" (*Queen Mom: A Royal Plan for Restoring Order in Your Home* [Cincinnati, OH: Standard Publishing, 2007], 123). This truth is true for all wives, whether or not we ever have children. We are the heart of the home. Since women by nature are usually more relational, we are the ones who keep daily life going and relationships growing. Without the lifeblood we provide, the marriage can quickly go from two living in unity (Matthew 19:5, 6) to two living separate lives, thereby not fulfilling God's plan.

I know this may sound cavemanlike in our feminist, politically correct society. But, hey, I always tell people I feel like Wilma Flintstone. Take a look at my picture on my Web site (www.brendagarrison.com). See any resemblances? Hmm, maybe I look more like Lucille Ball in her *I Love Lucy* phase! No matter how old-fashioned we might (or might not) look, the truth is we must stick with God's truth and not the common wisdom of current culture. The wise wife nurtures her man and, as we discussed in chapter one, by so doing will be on the receiving end of the blessings of a rich marriage.

In Proverbs 31:10-31, we see our friend the Proverbs 31 woman (we've said good-bye to the Shulammite woman till chapter seven) doing much to take care of her husband—so much so that he trusts her and praises her (vv. 10, 11, 28-30):

A wife of noble character who can find?
    She is worth far more than rubies.

Her husband has full confidence in her
    and lacks nothing of value.

. . .

Her children arise and call her blessed;
    her husband also, and he praises her:

"Many women do noble things,
    but you surpass them all."

Charm is deceptive, and beauty is fleeting;
but a woman who fears the LORD is to be praised.

The adjective used to describe her (*virtuous*, *noble*, or *excellent*, depending on your translation) means "a force, whether of . . . an army, virtue, valor, strength" (*Strong's Exhaustive Concordance of the Bible*, 50, Hebrew and Chaldee Dictionary of the Old Testament). This wife is not to be messed with. Just try throwing the women's lib gospel at her and see how far you get. She knows the importance of her role in the home and she does it with purpose and dignity.

She blesses her husband by being a strong woman in many ways:

> ### If This Is You, Get Thee to Cooking School
>
> The pans you received for a wedding gift are still in the box in the basement. Your parents' basement. Three states away.
>
> You order "the usual" at all the local fast-food restaurants. And they actually know what you mean.
>
> The recipe told you to "simmer for 30 minutes." So you did just that—getting hotter by the second while your food got colder. Why didn't anyone say how to turn the stupid burner on?

⊙ She gives him no reason to distrust her (v. 11).

⊙ She does good things for him, nothing to hurt him (v. 12).

- She takes care of the home and the business of running it (vv. 14, 15, 27).

- She is a hard worker. She is not lazy (vv. 15, 17, 18, 19, 24, 27).

- She is a wise businesswoman (vv. 16, 24).

- She takes good care of her family and household (vv. 15, 21).

- She has strength of character and brings her husband honor (vv. 11, 23, 25).

The Proverbs 31 woman is her husband's go-to girl in every way. She takes good care of her man. When you take care of your man you help him be all God designed him to be. He knows he can depend on and trust you. You're it, girl. You're the one God has shaped to complete your man. So go stick your best bone in your hair and whip up some gravelberry pie—make Fred happy to come home to you.

{ Three Simple Phrases Sure to Make Your Man Smile }

Dinner's ready.

I believe in you, babe.

Dessert's ready.

to Being Fabulous

The smart girl designs a home with . . .

- ⊙ *A stable, yet flexible foundation.* Jill shared with me the story of the challenging beginning to their marriage. "Within one year we saw two career changes, two bouts of house damage that brought a two-month stay in a local hotel, both cars in the shop at the same time—all on top of a busy schedule and lots of travel. For a self-proclaimed planner, I've learned that creating a safe refuge for my husband means being adaptable, calm, and flexible no matter our location or life state. . . . I learned that my husband does not need a dust-free home but he does need a wife who is going to consistently encourage him, remain emotionally stable when things don't go as planned and be willing to do things that might not seem logical to me but show that I am here to push through the chaos with him."

- ⊙ *Free space.* Anna and her husband, John, have been in full-time ministry most of their nine-year marriage. "One of the best ideas I ever came up with was to force John to take a day out by himself. . . . Sometimes all he needs is a morning. . . . He comes back totally refreshed and ready to be fully engaged in family life. I try not to ask him to do anything while he's out, and I don't expect him home at any particular time. Sometimes these men who love us so well just need a chance to breathe, with no obligations to be anywhere, do anything, remember anything, or solve any crises. This has made a huge difference in our marriage, and he would encourage all guys to do it!"

⊙ *Comfort.* Another young wife who is on the mission field with her husband shared a basic but important way to take care of her husband. "My husband likes a neat and clean home (not perfect or sparkling clean—he is not a clean freak), and he enjoys a good meal. He works hard and his job is often physically demanding, so he appreciates good home-cooking. Coming home from work to a clean home and a meal already prepared helps with his sense of order and our family's schedule for the evening. I keep things running smoothly. I take care of many tasks for our work (missions) that he can't always find time to do (correspondence with supporters and churches, etc.)."

⊙ *Strong supports.* If you both work outside the home, or even if not, decide together who will do what jobs. Maybe your husband is a great cook, but stinks at managing money. Or maybe you have wonderful landscaping skills, but are terrible at grocery shopping. Making these decisions before the jobs need doing can relieve stress and strengthen the partnership between you and your husband.

- *Room to dream.* Does your husband have a dream? Is he currently finishing school so he can pursue his dream? A young wife, Jennie, explains how she supports her husband's dream. "I know that by being his biggest cheerleader and finding ways to infuse myself into his dream it won't become something that brings division between us, nor will someone else ever be able to step into that role in my place. I am more understanding of the time that is needed to make it work and see his dream grow. I constantly ask him about ways that I can help, be involved, and what he enjoys best about me being there. I know that my presence is not just about supporting him, but also honoring God through our marriage so that others can see me as his wife who is actively participating in his dream and his ministry."

- *A man cave.* It may be a corner of the garage or a workshop in the basement or a spare office space. Your man may cherish a room (no matter how small) that has not been decorated by you, where he can watch his own shows, catch up on his e-mail, and/or display his, uh, stuff—whatever that may be. Gene has a workshop in the basement and, don't you know, that is the first place he takes a first-time male visitor to our home. In my eyes it's a mess (sawdust accents every surface), but it's his pride and delight. It's a place where the guys can hang out and not worry about using coasters.

And one more thing on this point: Guys need something to call their own. If it's not breaking your bank or hurting family time, don't make a big deal about his toy(s). Gene has always had an inexpensive (piece of junk) sports car. The current one has only made it out of the garage a couple times in the past year. I've heard wives complain about stuff taking up space and nag their men to get rid of it. But really, is that wise? I can't help thinking that if men can be men at home, then they'll have no need to go elsewhere. Just saying.

chapter six

be his *what*?!

"I thought he said helper, not 'Help HER'!?!"

Are you hanging in there? Is marriage more than you expected? Sure, it's great to share a home, see each other every day, and have sex, but growing the marriage can be work. Hard work. Again, let me encourage you. Gene and I have been married twenty-five years, and at times I thought an alien had taken over his body. *What was he thinking anyway?* Gene, too, has wondered how to turn down the hormones that transformed his fairly calm wife into someone (or something) he didn't even recognize. But we stayed committed to each other and worked through the insanity. And it has been worth it.

One way we wives can live out our commitment to our men and live through the hard times is by fulfilling our role as helpers. Shudder. Yep, even now those words—*his helper*—give me visions of a suppressed, weak woman whose life is submerged in servitude to her husband. But if you know your Bible at all, or if you've lived longer than a week, you know this wasn't God's plan. Far from it.

The first mention of the role of a wife is at creation, when God declared the need for Eve. "The LORD God said, 'It is not good for the man to be alone'" (Genesis 2:18). God said it first and best—men need us! We complete our men. Our first role as wives is to be companions to our husbands.

My girls are thrilled I have the opportunity to speak on the weekends, but they cringe when they think about how Gene handles my absences. Sure, he supports me 1000 percent, but when I'm gone he misses me. He teeters between being supermom and lonely bachelor. He attacks the laundry like a Marine taking no prisoners in a battle. Then every thirty minutes or so he asks the girls if their homework is done (even after it is done). Finally, he retreats to his man cave to watch his man shows and eat PayDay candy bars. It's *so* "not good for the man to be alone." The man needs his woman.

The second role mentioned in Genesis is that of helper:

"I will make a helper suitable for him." Now the LORD God had formed out of the ground all the beasts of the field and all the birds of the air. He brought them to the man to see what he would name them; and whatever the man called each living creature, that was its name. So the man gave names to all the livestock, the birds of the air, and all the beasts of the field. But for Adam no suitable helper was found. So the LORD God caused the man to fall into a deep sleep; and while he was sleeping, he took one of the man's ribs and closed up the place with flesh. Then the LORD God made a woman from the rib he had taken out of the man, and he brought her to the man. (Genesis 2:18-20)

You know I'm crazy curious, so I looked up the definition of *helper* in these verses. It comes from a word that means "to surround, protect, or aid." Don't you love it? All these strong, independent, brave, manly men—what do they need? To be surrounded, protected, aided—*helped*—by a good woman. This is no job for a suppressed, weak servant. This is the work of a fully engaged, confident, life–giving partner.

Those actions of the woman in Proverbs 31 surround her home, her marriage, her man with protection. Everything we've talked about

{ **You Know Your Husband Misses You When . . .** }

Yyou pull in the driveway and the first thing you see is your husband's face pressed against the window.

Yyou find him sitting in a dark room watching your wedding video and wearing your veil.

He puts his name in your calendar for lunch on Wednesday. And Thursday, Friday, Saturday, Sunday . . .

so far—being your man's go-to girl—is for the purpose of surrounding your man with protection. When you are his go-to girl in every area, you give him the affirmation, romance, appreciation, encouragement, conversation, companionship, and physical affection (hang on—chapter seven is next!) he needs. He doesn't have to look anywhere else—he's surrounded by you. You are keeping him safe in God's will and growing your marriage.

The other definition of *helper* is "to aid." We are to provide useful assistance to our husbands so they can achieve their goals. For years I have tried to assist Gene in home

{ The Go-To Girl Flies to the Aid of Her Husband By. . . }

Reminding him of his parents' anniversary and handing him the phone with their number already dialed.

Planning for his game day—complete with tailgate food, team jerseys, and face paint.

Rescuing him from such sticky situations as missing socks, the delicate cycle, and shopping with your mother.

repairs, but—how can I say this nicely—Gene doesn't want my help. He isn't rude to me, but when he's fixing things, an invisible workspace bubble forms around him. I just *know* I shouldn't come too close. So I asked him what it is that I do for him that *is* helpful. The thing he found most helpful was how I listen to him talk about his day and different situations in his day and then offer my perspective on how the situation or person might be dealt with. Although he doesn't always do what I suggest, I give him a different perspective that helps him come up with his approach. After all, I'd rather talk than hold a wrench any day.

Whether or not he has home repairs to make, your man needs your help. Be proud to be the only "suitable helper" for him. And if you don't know where he needs your help the most, that's easy. Just ask him!

the SMART GIRL'S GUIDE to Being Fabulous

Smart girls know how to protect, help, and pour into their men.

⊙ *Be involved.* Zoe literally put the rubber to the road to support her man's passions. "I took up running for that reason, and even though I don't run as much as he does, I've done three half marathons and many shorter races. I got scuba certified, something I love, but I doubt I would have been motivated to do it except that it was his absolute passion. I know next to nothing about sports, but since he is a huge sports fan, I learn the names of some of the major team members of his favorite teams and enough about the sports lingo that I don't have to ask annoying questions after every play! I also clip news articles for him about his teams. He reciprocates this too—he can quote almost any line of Mr. Darcy in both film versions of *Pride and Prejudice!*"

⊙ *Be available.* Our husbands love to have us around—they wouldn't have married us if they didn't. You can't be his companion if your schedule is too full of work, shoe shopping, or Facebook. Married couples need to hang out together. How else will you learn to complete each other's sentences and grow to look like each other? (See what I mean by looking at the picture of Gene and me on my Web site!) I have infinite memories of my mom sitting in the lawn chair while my dad worked on one of our cars (us kids always drove a second- or thirdhand car!). Yep, she always had a million other things to do, but she knew the importance of simply hanging out with her man. Fifty-one years later, they are still hanging out together—every morning they go to Panera for coffee.

◉ *Be on the lookout.* My friend Luci and her husband are missionaries in Africa. They do not have a physically present support team of friends and family so they truly do need to help each other. Luci shared this, "We discussed how we help each other and George simply concluded, 'We make a good team.'" Just ask how you can help. Luci went on, "We both look to help the other person. We even ask if the other needs help, wants something, etc."

◉ *Be there to pick up his load.* Jenna's husband is a CPA. "He handles all the bookkeeping, taxes, etc., which I dread like the plague. But once in a while, he's swamped and asks me to enter data into Quicken or write and mail some checks." Jenna is wisely investing in her marriage.

◉ *Be in prayer.* Caroline shared with me the most important way to help our men—one we often forget. "I pray that God would give him peace, keep him pure from sin, give him purity in regards to external values, protect him from evil, for help in enhancing his own intimacy with God—praying for his perseverance to the end, that his motivation to do what is right would remain strong and solid! I may be able to pull off many things to aid my husband, but I really do not have any claim to power. I need to rely on God's power to bless and protect my husband!" She added, "I must also pray for myself. If my heart is not right, I will sabotage my own prayers for my husband!"

chapter seven

crockpot,
meet microwave

"C'mon, Linda, you're killin' me! Remember?
48-hour lifespan?"

I am the oldest of five sisters. I have no brothers. So I was quite naive about the inner thought processes and ways of men. Day One of our marriage was the beginning of my twenty-five years in "Man Class." I am still learning what makes my man tick, but the most surprising fact I have learned is how differently men and women think about sex. It's almost as if they speak different languages—neither understands the other but strangely enough, they both believe the other side must know exactly what they are thinking. Think about it. Women think men know when the time is right, so they shouldn't have to drop any clues. Men think the time is always right and therefore women ought to always be ready.

Unfortunately much of what young men and women think they know about sex has come from the world. This interpretation of sex is not accurate because, for one thing, it is not portrayed in the context of healthy marriage, which was God's *only* design for sex since the first married couple. Many of us did not have a godly older woman share with us about men's sex language and how we can speak it back to them. So consider me your godly older woman. I'll share with you a little of what I have learned in Man Class.

Everything we discuss in this book is not only vital for laying the foundational first year of marriage, but continuing to build in these areas will help to grow a marriage that lasts a lifetime. The sexual part of a relationship cannot be underestimated. It is important not only when you are just starting out, but all through your marriage. As your lives get busier and fuller, the first part of your relationship you will be tempted to neglect is the sexual part. I know you can't imagine this happening to you and your beloved. But it will.

The act of sex brings you together in unity as nothing else can or does. Satan wants to destroy the perfect, holy union God made in your marriage. The easiest way to get a wedge between the two of you is in your physical relationship. It's no surprise to find Paul writing on this very subject in his first letter to the Corinthians: "The husband should fulfill his marital duty to his wife, and likewise the wife to her husband. The wife's body does not belong to her alone but also to her husband. In the same way, the husband's body does not belong to him alone but also to his wife. Do not deprive each other except by mutual consent and for a time, so that you may devote yourselves to prayer. Then come together again so that Satan will not tempt you because of your lack of self-control" (7:3-5).

Sex is a *big* deal to men not only physically, but emotionally. In *For Women Only*, Shaunti Feldhahn states, "Lack of sex is as emotionally serious to him as, say, his sudden silence would be to you, were he simply to stop communicating with you" (92). Sex not only unites you as a couple, but it affirms your man. Loving your man through sex *shows* him he is your big, hairy man. With Gene's permission I share this—his humor is always a little cornier, and his smile a bit wider the day after. Loving, passionate, respectful sex in marriage builds up a husband like nothing else can—no promotion, new car, or big-screen TV.

> ### Lost in Translation
>
> You say: "You look great in your new suit."
>
> He hears: "She wants me."
>
> You say: "Thanks for picking up the dry cleaning."
>
> He hears: "She wants me."
>
> You say: "Would you mind doing the dishes tonight?"
>
> He hears: "She wants me."

As I wrote this chapter, I called Gene at work (remember, he works in construction so he had privacy to take my call—on a large job site with heavy equipment running) to see what he thought I should make sure to include. He called back and reminded me of something from our premarital counseling. He said, "I remember a statement from a book [that we used in the counseling], 'Intimacy begins with sharing something intimate.' So there needs to be preparation."

For each couple this will be unique. Recently Gene and I had an evening out—nothing glamorous. We like to start in the late afternoon. We shopped at a local antique shop and bought two unique, inexpensive pieces that need Gene's tender, loving refinishing. Then we had dinner at our favorite restaurant and finished the evening by going to a home improvement store to get paint for one of the pieces of furniture. Not fancy, but we had a great time doing what we both love. Spending time together doing something you both enjoy can be great preparation for other activities you both will enjoy. A few more ideas to prepare yourselves are:

- Have a nice dinner where you can talk and actually hear each other.

- Watch a classic romantic comedy together. Laughing together can be a very intimate experience. And who doesn't enjoy Cary Grant?

- Spend time in God's Word together. Stumped for where to start? How about Song of Songs?

- Discuss and work through an issue that you have been avoiding. Really, nothing is more intimate than when you get through to each other's hearts.

Perhaps the most important thing to remember here is stated in the title of this book. He's not a mind reader. And he certainly doesn't think like you. You will need to communicate to him what works for you in your sexual relationship. Start with letting him know what gets you in the mood—and what doesn't.

I've heard this comparison made regarding the sexual differences in men and women—men are like microwaves and women are like crockpots. This analogy may be life-changing for your husband (that is, if he knows anything about crockpots—you might need to start there). He might not understand that you need time to "warm up." He may interpret your inability to transition from bill paying to passionate sex in less than thirty seconds as rejection.

What he needs to know is that all you need is a hot shower (I hate baths), a chick flick (at least part of one), and a massage and you are ready. Or whatever works for you. One wife I know said that she has explained to her husband that sex for her starts at least twenty-four hours before the main event—the positive things her husband says to her, the little things he does around the house, the help he gives her during that time. All these things can contribute to a woman's ability to get in the mood. But he may never catch on to this, no matter what his IQ, unless you tell him.

For example, if most of the household chores fall to you, you might suggest to him that if you had help with the laundry you would have more energy and time for *other* things later. Just try not to laugh as he folds the towels at warp speed and power walks through the house, hanging undies up in the closet and shoving dresses into drawers.

{ Three Things
That Tell Him Your
Crockpot Is Unplugged }

You're wearing your fuzzy socks to bed.

There's a forest growing on your legs.

The bed is covered with unpaid bills.

The microwave image for men is probably more often true than not. However, women also need to be sensitive to what works best (or definitely doesn't) to put their men in the mood. And yes, even guys get headaches sometimes.

Sex is the invisible bond between a husband and wife. It sweetens and matures the relationship. If it is made a priority and nurtured, it grows stronger and more precious with time. Kind of like a really good stew in a crockpot (note: really good stew has also been known to put men in the mood).

to Being Fabulous

S mart girls learn how to keep things cooking.

- *Be intentional.* A young wife of eight years shared a practical and wise idea. "We have to be creative about having date nights, because the work is never done. But if we have a rendezvous set up, it's exciting. Plus I try to mentally shift from sex being one more thing I have to do to sex being a little getaway and an escape." I love her attitude!

- *Talk!* A young wife and her husband shared with me how they have learned each other's sex language. "Once I told John that I heard, 'Talking is to a woman, like sex is to a man.' To which he replied, 'Let's talk!' He knows the more I talk and connect with him in that way, the more I will be in the mood!"

- *Let him know he's on your mind.* Another wife shared with me an idea for the "preparation" part of sex. Her husband loves it when she takes a picture of herself in lingerie and puts it in a place where only he will find it.

- *Create sacred space.* As much as possible, save your bedroom only for sleeping and sex. Keep it clutter-free and clean. I know this is hard. Especially as newlyweds, your first place most likely is small and rooms need to do double duty. Do your best to make your bedroom a retreat. Add inexpensive touches to make it romantic, but not feminine. For years Gene suffered through purple flowers everywhere in our room. In my defense, they were the style for a while. Now we love a more neutral color palette, candles, and comfy pillows.

- *Select the right packaging.* Wear lingerie or sleepwear that looks good on you. As with all clothing choices, certain styles look better on our bodies than others. Usually what we feel best and most confident wearing is going to be the best choice. Buy what looks best on you and what you feel the sexiest in. If it makes you feel cheap, don't buy it (or if it was a gift, get rid of it). And don't forget to get his opinion. Even his old football jersey can be sexy if that's what he likes to see you wearing.

- *Protect your man.* Respect your man and your marriage by keeping the details of your sex life private. "Marriage should be honored by all, and the marriage bed kept pure, for God will judge the adulterer and all the sexually immoral" (Hebrews 13:4). Here God instructs us not only to stay faithful to our husbands but to honor our marriages. In fact, he states that marriage is to be honored by everyone. So resist the temptation to blab regarding your intimate relationship. Many women betray their husbands in this way. Flee from these conversations. Your man and your marriage are priceless. Do whatever it takes to protect them.

chapter eight

he's not your dad,
you're not his mom

Monday: Sue meets Bob's parents.
Tuesday: Sue schedules premarital counseling.

At a bridal shower I recently attended, the bride opened her gift from the groom's mother and found an apron with the two ties neatly snipped off. That was all that was in the box. Her future mother-in-law explained, "This was my apron. Daniel cut off the apron strings and now they are yours."

I broke into *vigorous* applause, which quickly ended because I was the only one clapping! But I meant every loud, lonely clap that echoed between houses (it was a garden shower). What a wise groom and future mother-in-law! Both mother and son knew that for the couple's marriage to thrive the newlyweds would need to start their own individual family, putting each other above all the rest.

It's the simple but profound leave-and-cleave concept that Jesus taught in Matthew 19:5. Jesus quoted his Father in answer to the Pharisees' question on divorce: "For this cause shall a man leave father and mother, and shall cleave to his wife: and they twain shall be one flesh" (*KJV*).

We don't use the word *cleave* much, but the definition is "to glue to; to adhere" (*Strong's Exhaustive Concordance of the Bible*, 82,

Hebrew and Chaldee Dictionary of the Old Testament). If you have ever glued your fingers together, you know there is no room between them for even a thin, sharp blade to separate them without danger of cutting one or both fingers. That is how close we are to be as husband and wife. We are to be so close that nothing or no one can get a smidge between us.

I did not do well in this area in the first few years of my marriage. I thought my dad knew everything (it's irrelevant if he did or not). I don't know how I missed the fact that, even before I met Gene, he had lived a full life—after an off-and-on nontraditional childhood (which taught him street smarts) he went to college, then the Vietnam War, then back to college, and then to work. He had rich life experiences that I did not give him credit for. Yes, it caused tension in our marriage. I don't remember when or how the change came, but gradually God showed me how wrong I had been. I then acknowledged Gene as my go-to guy and treated him that way. Our relationship flourished.

If your husband is having trouble leaving his mom or still favors his mom over you, find a time when you both are relatively relaxed and talk to him about this. Share with him what you experience and how it makes you feel. A dear friend has worked hard in her twenty years of marriage to build a relationship with her mother-in-law while keeping healthy boundaries. Her situation includes more than one difficult, boundary-pushing circumstance that would send most of us into the fetal position within a few days. Get this—she lives in her mother-in-law's former home and her in-laws built a house right next door! What follows are several of her valuable insights (names have been changed to protect the innocent . . . and the in-laws).

She confessed, "I think the biggest thing for me has been establishing boundaries. Since I live next door to my mother-in-law, boundaries have been so important, but painful, because Dave and I both hate conflict. If we didn't have to do it, it would be easier to just avoid. But we have to address boundaries for my sanity and honestly, so my mother-in-law and I can have a good and healthy relationship. I firmly established the boundaries of where she could 'intrude' in our life, and because she's right next door that meant getting

> {
> **Three (or Four) Ways to Destroy Mother-In-Law/ Daughter-In-Law Harmony**
> }
>
> Refer to her as "the other woman."
>
> Cut her out of your wedding pictures.
>
> Send her clothing gifts that are all three sizes too big.
>
> Be critical of her behind her back when talking to your mother, your neighbor, the family dog, etc.

specific about visiting rules and when and how she could enter our house!

"While being assertive and brutally honest, I have also tried to show her love. I can say I have a really good relationship with her. One way I've tried to show her love is to make 'deposits' with her when I can. I invite them to dinner, invite them on weekend trips with us, and give them tickets for our church's huge Easter cantata, taking them out to dinner afterward. Dave always makes sure they know it was my idea (when it was).

"I have blessed her by intentionally forcing myself to ask her for help with cooking/recipes and gardening issues. It doesn't seem like much, but cooking and gardening are her passions, and I have to humble myself to ask questions. She lights up when I do. It sounds crazy, but I have to fight the impulse to give her the impression I can do everything and am completely self-sufficient. She is an excellent seamstress and once tried to teach me to sew and gave me an old sewing machine. Later I tried to just cut up an old towel and serge the edges to make cleaning rags. It was a disaster (again, couldn't humble myself and call for help). The thread was knotted and tangled. I was laughing at myself by the end. It looked so pathetic that I couldn't keep the joke to myself, and as an exercise in humility, I wrapped the sorry scrap as a gift for her. I included a note that said, 'Thanks for all the sewing and alterations you do for me!' We had a good laugh at my attempt at sewing—something as simple as that really helped thaw our relationship."

I think you can see from what she said that the key is to have a healthy balance of humility and pride. Be proud of your man, your marriage, your home—don't apologize for your need to protect and care for your family unit. But at the same time, be humble. Realize that (at least in many cases) there are some parents who, for better or worse, poured a large portion of their time, heart, sweat, and tears into the man you call your husband, and give them the respect they deserve.

{ Duct Tape Your Mouth
If These Words
Come to Mind }

Dad never does it that way.

Dad always buys a Ford.

You're just like your mother.

If you are living with a particularly sticky situation, or if your man just doesn't get where you are coming from, you may want to return to your premarital counselor to discuss your in-law relationships. If your husband is resistant to counseling, consider going yourself. Whatever you do, don't ignore the issues.

You could try sweeping your in-laws under the rug, but I think that's illegal in most states. And besides, good relationships with your family and your husband's family can add richness to your lives.

S mart girls work to make their in-law relationships thrive.

⊙ *Don't compare your husband* to your dad or anyone else's dad. Your dad has his strengths and so does your man. List your husband's good (even unique) qualities, character traits, and habits. Pick the one you appreciate the most. Would you consider trading it for a good quality in any other man? (The right answer here is no!)

⊙ *Your dad is not your 411 or 911.* Don't call Dad first for advice: home repairs, buying a car, house, etc. Let your man work it out. Talk it through as a couple. If he wants advice, he knows your dad's phone number.

⊙ *He's not your dad.* This statement is perhaps even more important for those women who did not have the best male role model as they were growing up. Don't project your dad's shortcomings onto your husband.

⊙ *You're not his mom.* Don't feel pressured to do everything the way his mommy did it. You need to make your own way. But do ask your husband to help you understand your mother-in-law's customs and background. When we were first married my mother-in-law (remember—a farm wife) asked me if I needed any more "bed clothes." I thought she wanted to give me a few of her "old lady" nightgowns. I immediately, but graciously, declined. When I told Gene about our conversation he enlightened my city-girl vocabulary, "Bed clothes are sheets and blankets!" My mother-in-law was trying to gift me with bed linens and I thought she wanted me to wear her nightgowns! Oops.

- ⊙ *Be realistic.* List your husband's weaker areas—especially considering things he has "inherited" or that came from his family/childhood culture. Yes, I mean it. This is not to pick on him or man-bash him—while you're at it, list yours too! Now both of you can manage your expectations. Gene spent many of his growing-up years on a farm. The cliché is true—you can take the boy out of the farm but you can't take the farm out of the boy. Since farmers work outside with agriculture all day, most of them don't enjoy landscaping as a hobby. This is true of Gene. He will do whatever I ask for landscaping projects, even help me design and implement our ideas, but Gene's fun is not manicuring the lawn, as a couple of my friends' husbands love to do. I finally figured this out and learned to be very pleased with all the help Gene gives me, not expecting more.

- ⊙ *Plan ahead.* Holidays are quite possibly one of the top-ten things that give married couples stress in their first years together. Whose family will you visit? What traditions do you keep? Do you celebrate on the day itself or on other days? Have an honest talk about this (and other important family events) with your husband long before the decorations start showing up in the grocery store. Find out what holidays and family traditions are dearest to each other and plan how you'll approach them together. Then stick to the plan. And remember, you're a family of your own now—start some of your own traditions!

- *Know when to keep your mouth shut.* A dear friend of mine is learning the best way to "communicate" with her mother-in-law. "My in-laws are fun, fantastic people. However, my mother-in-law has a habit of getting way too involved in everyone's business. I have had experiences where my mother-in-law will disagree with my husband regarding the way he does things, and then she calls me to work through me instead. I remain silent and just listen without defending my husband or myself. In other words, I do not dish out the information she is seeking. This makes her upset, but it is a smart pattern for me to continue until my in-laws get the message that what they are trying to control or receive information about is our business. It also shows that I respect my husband—who is a grown man, I might add!"

- *Overlook, don't overreact.* Natalie is a spunky young wife whose personality is very different from her mother-in-law's. She shares, "I have great in-laws. But there have been a few times when my feelings were inadvertently hurt by them. This has caused a lot of tension with my husband and myself. The only advice I have is not to hold your husband responsible for the way his family treats you. It's not his fault. I am not talking major areas of wrongs, but I am talking about learning to let some things go. . . . As Proverbs says, 'A wise man overlooks an offense'" (Proverbs 17:9; 19:11).

- ⊙ *Bless your mother-in-law with a new daughter.* Many mothers are thrilled to have a new "daughter" to help fill in the blanks in their sons' lives. Initiate contact with your mother-in-law. Recognize your in-laws' birthdays and anniversary.

- ⊙ *Work at it.* Turning in-laws to in-loves doesn't happen by magic. Developing friendships while establishing boundaries can be super difficult. For such situations I highly recommend *Boundaries: When to Say Yes, When to Say No to Take Control of Your Life*, by Drs. Henry Cloud and John Townsend (Grand Rapids, MI: Zondervan Publishing, 1992).

chapter nine

talking dollars and sense

"Budget's done. The good news is we can start eating out again in 2017!"

Fifty-seven percent of divorces in the United States were caused by financial problems (http://findarticles. com/p/articles/mi_m1355/is_nl_v91/ai_18930297/ [accessed 11.09.09]). I hate to start this chapter with such a dark cloud, but that statistic shows us what an important role our finances play in our marriages. But it's more than our finances—it's how each spouse feels about money that needs the attention and discussion.

One of my favorite cartoons when I was a kid was the Jetsons. (Yes, there was TV—even color TV—when I was a child!) Every week the show started with the theme song (hum it if you know it!) and the family starting their day. George, Jane, and their two children—Judy and Elroy—flew off to their destinations in the family's flying car. Jane was the last to be delivered to the shopping mall. George opened his wallet to give her one bill, but she grabbed the wallet and left him with the one bill. As a child I wondered, *Is that how it's done?*

Gene and I both came into marriage uninformed about how to handle money as a married couple. We stumbled through the first few years, then about year four we were hit by a financial tsunami. We had to learn quickly how to deal with it or we would go under. In October, 1988, I was pregnant with our second child (due in February, 1989) when Gene came home one day with bad news. "I'm laid off and they don't plan on bringing me back." He was discouraged and in disbelief, as I was.

I usually have lots of questions and comments, but this time there was nothing to discuss. Gene was out of work. We both knew, since it was late in the year, there were no construction jobs. I knew he felt the desperateness of the situation, so I backed off and gave him room to think and work through it.

We immediately went on unemployment and, even though it was helpful to have *something*, our income dropped dramatically. We needed a plan soon and we both needed to be on board with it or our finances (and potentially our marriage) would not survive.

> **Blatant Imitation of a Successful Ad Campaign to Make My Point**
>
> Daily lunches and dinners on nights you don't feel like cooking = five years of 20 percent interest for meals consumed in an hour.
>
> Buying a home = every stinkin' penny you earn.
>
> Jamaican vacation with best friends = maxed-out credit card and damaged credit score.
>
> Financial freedom and a fulfilling marriage = priceless.
>
> There are some things money can't buy; for everything, there's debt.

Situations like this can make or break a marriage. No one wants to consider the possibility of facing financial difficulties, but most of us will go through them at least once in our marriages. Even if you never have a worry about how you will make your house payment or about the security of your job, differences in how each spouse views and handles money can cause turmoil in the relationship. (Don't forget the dark cloud of fact that hovered over the start of this chapter.) I think it's no accident that directly after the counsel about keeping the marriage bed pure, the writer of Hebrews advises: "Keep your lives free from the love of money and be content with what you have, because God has said, "Never will I leave you; never will I forsake you" (13:5).

The key in handling financial issues (and all of marriage) starts with clear communication. Then you can make a plan and work at it together. Several weeks ago I experienced one of those times when you know God is telling you something. And that something is for you. Within one week two women—one a friend, one a business associate—told me of newly discovered financial troubles in their marriages. Their stories were almost identical: each couple kept two separate accounts. Each wife paid the household expenses from her account. Their husbands used their own accounts for non-household or bigger expenses—gifts, vacations, Christmas, etc. One husband also used his account for business expenses. These women have good marriages and each trusted her husband with his account and did not ask to see it. Then, without warning and by accident, each woman found her husband's deception. For most of their ten-year marriage one husband had gambled away close to $1,000,000. The other husband hid a maxed-out credit card in his account. Both marriages were rocked—one to the brink of divorce.

It is trendy and progressive to keep two accounts, especially since many couples have two incomes. However, two separate accounts can lead to the temptation of deception (women are just as guilty as men). You are one in God's sight. Keep the unity by keeping one account and keeping both of you fully informed of all financial transactions. Both of the previously mentioned couples are working hard to rebuild their finances and their marriages. But just think of all the emotional and relational expenses they might have been spared if they had simply kept a joint account.

Gene and I learned a lot the winter of 1988–89. We could barely make our bills on unemployment so Gene got two part-time jobs (earning the little allowed with unemployment). Also we came across a small booklet about budgeting (from Crown

Financial Ministries, www.crown.org). This was a new concept to us, but we learned what a budget was and put it into practice. Learning to budget and living within a budget is probably the most effective action we could have taken towards financial strength. It helped prepare us for the unexpected and make the best use of not only our regular income, but bonuses, inheritances, etc. That winter was an extremely tough time for us. But we came through it stronger as a couple and the parents of another beautiful red-haired daughter. In April 1989, Gene took a position with the company he has been with for twenty years. God is faithful. We just need to count on him.

{ Duct Tape Your Purse
If These Thoughts
Come to Mind }

But it's ON SALE!

Zero percent interest for six months—no problem!

No, I don't need a whole case of power bars, BUT I HAVE A COUPON!

Budget, smudget.

the SMART GIRL'S GUIDE to Being Fabulous

Smart girls know what adds up . . . and what doesn't.

- *Don't catch the affluenza bug* that is an epidemic in our country. When I look back and think over the things I thought I *had* to have, I can't think of one of those things that brought me lasting happiness. I have sent to Goodwill lots of stuff that I once thought was essential. Trust me—when you've been married twenty-five years and reflect on what gave you the most happiness and fulfillment, it won't be anything that once wore a price tag. There is nothing wrong with having stuff. It can add to our quality of life. But make sure your motives are right.

- *Money is not the goal.* Along the same line—don't get caught up in making money. Money is good and necessary in life, but the pursuit of it steals from the truly important. Instead invest in knowing God, serving him, and loving his people.

- *Live on one income.* If possible, learn to live on one income and use the second for saving (house, vacation, emergency funds, special acts of generosity, etc.). That way if/when something comes along that interrupts the flow of one paycheck, you will not be desperate. The interruption in income is fertile ground for stress in marriages. By not relying on both paychecks you have room for life's changes—both planned and unplanned.

◉ *Make a budget* or spending plan. Know how much comes in every month and how much goes out and where it goes. Both of you need to be aware of and understand the amounts of your expenses so everything can be planned for. A wise friend reminded me that our husbands are not mind readers regarding all that keeps their wives looking like the women they married. "If you have to have your hair highlighted every 6.25 weeks, tell him so it is not a surprise expense every other month."

◉ *Stick to the budget.* Don't hide purchases. Our friend, the Proverbs 31 wife, has the trust and confidence of her husband and he "lacks nothing of value" (v. 11). This would not be true if she spent the tent money on a new camel when the old one still rode fine. Develop your patience and wait for sales. Almost everything goes on sale in a matter of a few weeks. Deborah shared with me that at the beginning of their marriage, she and her husband made "no compromise" rules regarding saving and tithing.

⊙ *Live within your income.* Keep credit use to a minimum. My dear friends Bill and Cindy have a blended family of seven children—from high-school age to mid-twenties and married. "We adjust our lifestyle to fit our income through using a budget that we go over at the beginning of every month. We do not use any credit cards and pay cash for everything, including our cars. If the money is not there, the thing does not get bought. Such freedom comes with no debt—even our home is paid off! Needless to say, we sleep better at night. We have used the envelope system (cash) or our debit card. Either way we keep track of what we spend each month. My husband has an account with the Quicken program that when you use your debit card and pay for bills online it categorizes expenses, showing you how much you spent, and where and for what it was spent. By doing our finances this way, as a team, he sees what I spend and I see what he spends."

chapter ten

hang in there,
it's a process

"I'll tell YOU when the honeymoon is over!"

A few months ago I was hanging out with a friend as she cleaned her pool. I shared with her that I was about to start writing this book. Her first response was, "It's a process." She gently shook her head and chuckled, "I remember when I finally realized that it doesn't all have to be taken care of today."

Wow. What wisdom. I thought, *If every bride would realize this and then live it, the first few years of marriage would be way less stressful and way more fun.*

In our last few pages together I want to give you practical ways you can help your marriage and your man grow. For many of us wives, it is tempting to make our men our projects. I love the country song "I'm Still a Guy," sung by Brad Paisley. It tells the story of a wife bragging to her friends about how refined her husband is becoming under her tutelage. In the song the husband offers signs that he is evolving:

⊙ He writes her a love song.

⊙ He carries her purse while shopping.

⊙ He walks her tiny, foo-foo dog.

Of course, the chorus of the song reminds his wife that he is still a man and that he can change only so much.

Often the characteristics that first attracted us to our husbands now drive us crazy. I loved Gene's fun, easy-going personality when we were dating (and I still do). Then we became engaged. Since our engagement was only four months (really, what was I thinking?!) my Type A personality kicked into high gear. Suddenly Gene's laidback style was driving me crazy! It took time for me to appreciate this in Gene. Most times my STAT assessment of the situation was not shared by Gene. I learned to be more realistic about what needed to be taken care of and when. I also learned to give him as much lead time as I could so he could work my "emergency" into his schedule.

This is a great time to manage your expectations of your husband. First, list your expectations. (Don't go crazy here. Santa Claus won't be reading this.) Now look at each expectation and ask: Whose expectation is this? Did you inherit it from your dad? Maybe you absorbed it from your mom's comments? Maybe this was important in the church you grew up in. Have your friends handed you an unwritten list of how your husband should behave? Or maybe you've been listening to the voice of modern culture and now you're convinced you married the only surviving caveman. (Hey, if the loincloth fits . . .)

Go down your list and cross off—preferably in red pen to make an impact—the expectations that are not important to you. Do you really care if he washes both cars on Saturday morning just like Dad? Does it matter if he brings you flowers for no reason like your best friend's husband? Your man knows you would rather have a foot rub (have I mentioned how much I love a foot rub?) than flowers or shiny cars. Do you feel your man is not as spiritual as some because he doesn't pray out loud in group gatherings? Yet you know he doesn't compromise his faith on the job.

So what is left on your list? Do these items reflect what's truly important to you? If yes, how can you help your husband grow in these areas? Once I worked my way through my list (sorry to say, it took years— remember, it's a process for all of us),

{ Three Ways to Strangle the Process }

Tape an improvement chart on the fridge. Celebrate his areas of improvement with gold stars.

1. Place hand on hip.
2. Shake index finger, preferably in his face.
3. Using best motherly whine, state complaint. Works like a charm.

Nag, nag, nag. And nag some more. Did I say to nag? Nag.

decided what was truly important to me, and stopped making an issue of everything that I thought needed improvement, Gene was more eager to address the issues that mattered to me.

One more thing—the process of working through the list illuminated for me Gene's best qualities. I now value my man for who he is, unique from any other man. It's amazing how quickly criticisms shrink when they're not being fed by negative thoughts.

{ Take the Duct Tape Off and Say These Every Day }

What would I do without you!

Thank you!

I love you!

You're the man! You're the big, hairy man!

A dear young friend of mine and her husband are like Moose Tracks ice cream and vanilla ice cream—each with contrasting personalities. She shared with me how this process helped her when she was ready to light a rocket under his office chair and detonate his laptop. "It always helps me to sit back and remind myself of the reasons I was attracted and drawn to Tim in the first place. When I take the time to think back to the 'list' of things I adored about him (his stability, his consistency, his calm nature), I sigh and think, 'Oh, yes. I do love and need him.' Often the things that we once loved are the things that also drive us crazy."

Here's another list to consider: What dreams and goals does your husband have for himself or for you both as a couple? How can you help him in his process of becoming what God designed him to be?

No matter how primitive or out-of-sync you feel your husband is, he is still a man and he is still *your* man. Remember the words of 1 Peter 5:6: "Humble yourselves, therefore, under God's mighty hand, that he may lift you up in due time. Cast all your anxiety on him because he cares for you." Peter addressed these words to young men, but I think they are just as applicable to young women, or middle-aged and older women, as well. Don't worry so much, and don't take yourself so seriously. Put yourself in God's hands and let him do his work—on both of you.

the SMART GIRL'S GUIDE to Being Fabulous

S mart girls know how to hang.

- *Sow what you want to reap.* Our men have a tender part in their hearts that needs to be loved and affirmed. I'm not trying to put men down or make them sound weak. It's the truth. A wife's words can build her man up or tear him down (Proverbs 14:1; 15:4). Our critical words do not encourage our husbands to do better. Samantha learned this truth early in her marriage, "I always believe it's best to speak positively into my husband. Our words are seed, so if I am speaking negatively about him or to him, I'll get exactly what I've planted!"

- *Let him be the big, hairy man.* A precious young wife shared the following insight with me. Heidi writes, "God gave me a revelation early in my marriage that I believe helped us to move into our new lives as husband and wife smoothly. He reminded me that my husband cannot fulfill his role in our marriage if I am constantly doing it for him. Sometimes we get frustrated with our spouses because they are not doing something we feel they should. Maybe, just maybe, we need to take a step back and assess how we are allowing our men to fulfill their roles or if they're too busy trying to fight us for the position. It's been neat to see that with calm, clear communication and prayer for patience, my husband's confidence has increased and he steps up into his husband role just how I desire."

- *FYI—You're not the Holy Spirit.* A wife of ten years shared this revelation with me. She went on, "It took me a very long time to figure this out. There is nothing I will ever be able to do that will make him read his Bible more or lead with amazing prayers. The only thing I can do is pray for him and be affirming and encouraging when he does do these things. And he may never do them, so I have to accept that his spiritual walk may never resemble mine (I don't say amazing prayers, by the way). That doesn't mean that God isn't working in him. It just may look different. If I do shove it down his throat or criticize him in this area, it will embarrass him and push him even further away from ever sharing his spiritual life with me or anyone else."

- *Literally give him room to grow.* Create an atmosphere where the process can proceed. Men need a haven—a place to relax, to think, to be themselves. Emily shared with me how she learned this the hard way. "My husband works in a stressful, high energy, and noisy environment. . . . When we were going through a difficult trial in our marriage, I took every free minute to talk about and analyze the situation, including when he came home from work and right before he left for work. Not only did it make going to work stressful, it made coming home stressful. It was more than he could take and he told me so. I learned there is a right and wrong time to talk to him about stressful issues. I also need to do my best to create a warm, peaceful, food-filled place for him. It nourishes his soul. He needs his home to be a place where he can wind down and relax. I don't want him looking for that need anywhere else. I want him to want to come home."

⦿ *Keep going.* Sometimes marriage is really hard. And I'm not talking about fighting-over-where-to-eat-out kind of hard. I'm talking about soul-searching, mind-exhausting, depression-inducing kind of hard. But what would you expect from the most intense, deepest, closest, strongest relationship of your earthly life? The important thing to remember is you and your husband are not alone. People get married in front of witnesses for a reason. That reason should be to remind ourselves that marriage is a bond that is meant to be supported and encouraged and guarded by everyone: family, friends, pastors, counselors, and other married couples. Get help if you need it. Lean on each other. Love one another. And keep going . . . together.

conclusion

one more thing

"I'm not sure which one he is,
but we've been happily married for years."

pray for you a wonderful marriage. There is nothing comparable to doing life with your man through many, many years and experiences and knowing he is there for you no matter what. However, there are times when, for some couples, life together can fall far short of wonderful. It can be damaging. And no matter what a woman does or doesn't do, a husband may mistreat his wife. If you ever find yourself in this position, know this is not your fault. Please get help from someone who will help—trusted friends, pastors, counselors, women's shelters, law enforcement. If the first source doesn't help or won't listen, go on to the next. It is not God's will for you to be abused. You are not alone. You are his precious girl.

But for most couples, thankfully, the path they travel is not so dark. In most cases, the husbands don't have such serious, harmful, problems. And I hope, after reading this book, you've realized that it's not your job to change your man, and it's not his job to read your mind. But if you think your man could use a few hints about living with a woman, you might want to encourage him to check out the companion book to this one, *Put the Seat*

Down and Other Brilliant Insights for an Awesome First Year of Marriage, by Jess MacCallum.

The first year of marriage can be hard at times, sure. But it can also be exciting, fun, interesting, challenging, and . . . fabulous. So can the twenty-first year, or the fifty-first year. Take each day for what it is—don't expect perfection. But do embrace the life you have, and be thankful that you get to do it with the man who loves you. A journalist asked a couple married for fifty years what kept them together so happily for so long. The husband replied: "Besides loving each other, we're friends. . . . And when I wake up in the morning and I see her, I think, 'Another day. Thank God'" (said by Morty Kratem, in the article "Now That's Devotion," by Emily Tan, February 18, 2010, www.lemondrop.com).

So tomorrow, when you wake up, or whenever you next get to see your man's face, take a moment. Thank God for what you have. Then figure out what you can do to make this day of your marriage fabulous. Then keep doing that for, oh, the next 30,000 days. I promise it will be worth it.

about the author

Brenda Garrison is a wife, stay-at-home mom, author, and speaker who empowers women of all ages and backgrounds with the confidence to live their calling. Actively involved in leading women's ministries for over a decade, she speaks the truth of God's Word to women (including her three daughters) so they can live and be all God planned for

them to be. Brenda and her big, hairy man, Gene, have been married for over twenty-five years. They have a totally red-headed family—including their golden retriever, Riley—and live near Metamora, Illinois.

To find out more about Brenda and read her blog, go to www.brendagarrison. com. Brenda's other books include *Queen Mom: A Royal Plan for Restoring Order in Your Home* and *Princess Unaware: Finding the Fabulous in Every Day*. They can be purchased at www.standardpub.com.

Discover more brilliant insights on marriage and life in . . .

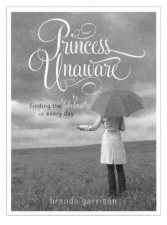

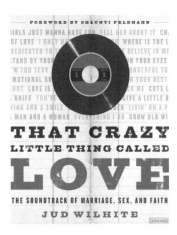

Also by Brenda Garrison!

Princess Unaware
Item #24340
ISBN 978-0-7847-2118-6

That Crazy Little Thing Called Love
Item #24311
ISBN 978-0-7847-1944-2

And be sure to grab this companion guide for the smart guy in your life.

Put the Seat Down and Other Brilliant Insights for an Awesome First Year of Marriage
Item #021536109
ISBN 978-0-7847-7462-5

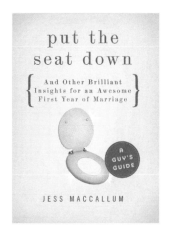

• • •

Visit your local Christian bookstore or
www.standardpub.com

Standard
PUBLISHING
www.standardpub.com